MW00533841

GUIDO GISLER

HIKING
IN SWITZERLAND
VIA ALPINA

Via Alpina 1

AT VERLAG

Publisher:
Swiss Hiking Federation
Monbijoustrasse 61
Postfach
3000 Bern 23
www.wandern.ch

English translation:
English Texts & Translations, Interlaken

© 2008
AT Verlag, Baden and Munich
Frontispiece: Christof Sonderegger, photo content: Guido Gisler
Map extracts: Kartographie und Grafik Schlaich, Geislingen
Lithographs: Vogt-Schild Druck, Derendingen
Printing and binding: AZ Druck und Datentechnik, Kempten
Printed in Germany

ISBN 978-3-03800-405-9

www.at-verlag.ch

Hiking in Switzerland

Dear Hikers

The Swiss Hiking Federation and its cantonal specialist hiking organizations offer you a warm welcome to «Hiking in Switzerland». They offer you a choice of the loveliest national and regional hiking routes, certain to gladden the heart of every hiker – for what could be more rewarding and refreshing than discovering Switzerland's wealth of nature and culture on foot? Whether as a tour of several days or a short one-day tour, the choice is enormous and covers the whole range of hiking options in Switzerland.

The Swiss Hiking Federation, since 1934 the umbrella organization of the specialist hiking organizations, is committed to maintaining an attractive, nationwide and safe network of hiking trails in Switzerland and the Principality of Liechtenstein that is signposted uniformly and without interruption. In the meantime, this network extends over more than 60 000 kilometres, the Swiss Hiking Federation, together with cantonal authorities and tourism partners, has selected the most beautiful national and regional hiking routes within the SwitzerlandMobility network and incorporated them into a grid of over 460 service locations. These service locations have public transport connections and a uniform standard in terms of services for hikers such as accommodation, catering and shopping possibilities. The service locations also serve as links for other forms of active recreation and leisure pastimes, such as cycling, mountain biking, skating and canoeing. Each of these forms of mobility has its uniformly designed route information panel on the signposts. The national routes are marked with one-digit numbers, the regional routes with two-digit numbers. For this reason, the classic yellow signposts for trails on «Hiking in Switzerland» routes have now been supplemented with yellow signposts with a green route information panel. Because hiking not only offers peace, recreation and a respite from the hectic pace of everyday life but also contributes to good health, it has experienced a Renaissance in recent years. The new services of «Hiking in Switzerland» will make hiking even easier – thus motivating the entire population to lace up their hiking boots.

The Swiss Hiking Federation is delighted to commit itself as an expert and reliable partner on all hiking matters and to enable every hiker to enjoy unique and unforgettable hikes.

The Swiss Hiking Federation – paving the path to your hiking excursions!

Schweizer Wanderwege
Suisse Rando
Sentieri Svizzeri
Sendas Svizras

A journey of discovery on 5000 kilometres of hiking trails in the Alps

The National Route 1 Via Alpina, is part of the Via Alpina long-distance hiking network linking Monaco on the Côte d'Azur with Trieste on the Adriatic. Over 5000 kilometres of hiking trails – split into 5 routes and 341 one-day stages – not only open up a breathtaking Alpine world but also link diverse living, cultural and natural environments and make hiking in Europe's largest area of unspoiled nature an exceptional journey of discovery.

Leading along existing hiking trails, the Via Alpina crosses a unique Alpine region, the largest area of unspoiled nature in Europe extending across eight Alpine countries – France, Italy, Monaco, Switzerland, Liechtenstein, Germany, Austria and Slovenia. But the Via Alpina also stands for a variety of cultural and scenic landscapes with an enormous number of species of flora and fauna, for history, togetherness and peace, tradition and culinary treats.

Via Alpina – a European project

Initiated by the French society La Grande Traversée des Alpes, GTA, the project has been implemented by institutions, associations and tourism organizations from the eight Alpine nations, including the Swiss Hiking Federation. The Via Alpina is an EU-backed project to support structurally weak regions and promote the Alpine identity. The route thus takes into account numerous political, environmental and touristic aspects. With over sixty border crossings, the Via Alpina underlines the common Alpine identity of the eight Alpine nations. Furthermore, it spotlights the importance of the Alps not only in terms of tourism but also as the endangered largest area of unspoiled nature in Europe. The project was financed by the European Fund for Regional Development as well as by financial assistance from the Swiss Federation, Interreg IIIB (joint initiative on cooperation in the field of spatial planning), the Swiss cantons and the Swiss Hiking Federation.

Through the Alps on established hiking trails

The Via Alpina hiking trails are mostly located at altitudes between 1000 and 3000 metres and are basically accessible from mid-June to mid-September. Stretches at lower altitudes are naturally open for much longer periods. Overall the route presents a medium degree of difficulty, avoiding climbing passages and glacier traverses. It comprises already established and signposted hiking trails that also display the Via Alpina logo. Hikers will find accommodation and refreshment possibilities at the finish of each one-day stage and grocery stores and other services are reached at regular intervals along the route.

Monaco, one of the endpoints on the Via Alpina

The Via Alpina in Switzerland

The red route of the Via Alpina is the actual backbone of the long-distance trail. With a total of 161 stages, it is the only one of the five routes to cross all eight Alpine countries. In Switzerland it begins at the border to the Principality of Liechtenstein, crosses the Lower and Upper Engadine, north Ticino, the Rhone valley and the Bernese Oberland to finally leave Switzerland in the Lower Valais over the Great St. Bernhard Pass. The green route runs in 14 stages from Vaduz over numerous Alpine passes to the Trütlisberg Pass near Lenk. The green and red routes run parallel from Adelboden to the Trütlisberg Pass. From the Trütlisberg Pass, you can either take the red route to Lauenen, the next stage stop on the way towards Monaco or the Via Alpina feeder leading in four stages to Montreux.

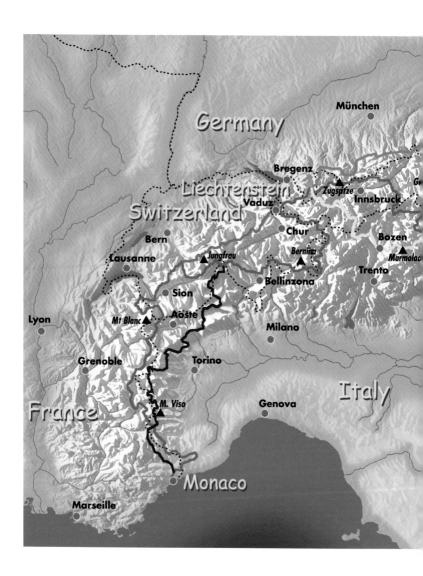

München

Germany

Bregenz

Zugspitze

Innsbruck

Gr

Liechtenstein

Vaduz

Switzerland

Chur

Bozen

Bern

Bernina

Marmolac

Lausanne

Jungfrau

Trento

Bellinzona

Sion

Milano

Mt Blanc

Aöste

Lyon

Grenoble

Torino

Italy

France

M. Viso

Genova

Monaco

Marseille

An overview of the Via Alpina

The Via Alpina consists of five sections with a total of 342 stages and around 5000 kilometres of hiking trails.

 Red trail: 161 stages linking Triest–Monaco through 8 countries

 Violet trail: 66 stages through Slovenia, Austria and Germany

 Yellow Trail: 40 stages through Italy, Austria and Germany

 Green trail: 14 stages through Liechtenstein and Switzerland

 Blue Trail: 61 stages through Switzerland, Italy and France

Information
www.via-alpina.org

Hiking in Switzerland

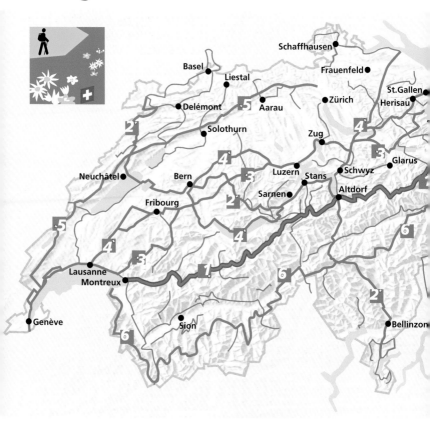

National routes in figures

1 Via Alpina
370 km
19 stages
24 400 metres height difference

2 Trans Swiss Trail
460 km
30 stages
16 500 metres height difference

SwissTrails

The national routes can be individually booked (accommodation and luggage transport) at www.swisstrails.ch or tel. +41 (0)44 450 24 34

5 Jura Crest Trail
310 km
15 stages
13 800 metres height difference

6 Alpine Passes Trail
600 km
34 stages
39 600 metres height difference

Regionale routes in figures

Volumes 7–9 offer a selection of the loveliest regional routes (thin green line on map). More information: www.wanderland.ch.

7 Highlights Kulturwege Schweiz
7 routes in 41 stages

3 Alpine Panorama Trail
510 km
30 stages
18 500 metres height difference

4 ViaJacobi
725 km
35 stages
19 800 metres height difference

8 Highlights West
19 routes in 67 stages

9 Highlights Ost
18 routes in 68 stages

The height difference in metres always refers to the hiking direction described in the volume.

Action-packed Switzerland

Switzerland is a natural paradise for active people – and with Switzerland-Mobility you can discover the most beautiful tours, through all parts of the country and to suit all tastes.

Our Internet site has information on routes, how to reach departure points by public transport, stage destinations and guest houses, route guides and bookable offers.

Take new paths to enjoy Switzerland.

SwitzerlandMobility

Hiking in Switzerland.

Through extensive forests, deep valleys, over scenic crests and beyond the horizon: SwitzerlandMobility has picked out the most beautiful routes from Switzerland's world-famous network of hiking trails; a total of 6300 hiking kilometres – the very best of Switzerland.

Cycling in Switzerland.

There are cyclists who like to take it easy. And sporty ones who seek their limits. Whether easy or energetic, over hours or days, SwitzerlandMobility's 8500 cycling kilometres offer ample variety to suit all tastes.

Mountain biking in Switzerland.

The spikes grip, gravity plays its part, your muscles ache and nature always has new delights in store: surprising, awe-inspiring, stunning. For freedom without end, SwitzerlandMobility recommends 3300 kilometres of mountain biking at its best.

Skating in Switzerland.

The exhilarating dance on rollers goes onwards, ever onwards, alongside lovely lakes, on easy downhill riverbank paths and across endless plains. SwitzerlandMobility has 1000 skating kilometres for your pleasure.

Canoeing in Switzerland.

Life is in full flow, especially with a trip by canoe or dingy on a wonderful stretch of water. To strike out for new shores, SwitzerlandMobility suggests 330 canoeing kilometres on idyllic rivers and picture-postcard lakes.

www.Switzerlandmobility.ch

www.hiking-in-switzerland.ch

www.cycling-in-switzerland.ch

www.mountainbiking-in-switzerland.ch

www.skating-in-switzerland.ch

www.canoeing-in-switzerland.ch

We bid you a warm welcome

Many hotels, camping sites, private rooms, youth hostels and farms have been awarded the SwitzerlandMobility Foundation quality label. All have made a notable commitment to meeting the wishes of hikers.
– Accommodation also possible for one night
– Washing and drying facilities for clothes and equipment
– Bath/shower facilities in rooms or on the premises
– Information on Hiking in Switzerland offers
– Provision of brochures on local touristic offers
All hiker-friendly establishments are listed in the SwitzerlandMobility Accommodation Guide (published by Werd Verlag) featuring the main services provided.

Hiker-friendly establishments can also be found with your mobile phone using BeeTaggs. See the following page and the BeeTagg list at the end of this book.

Water from public fountains in Switzerland may be consumed without hesitation; if not there will be a warning sign.

Hiker-friendly establishments are recognized by the SwitzerlandMobility quality label.

This guide is available at book stores or from Hiking in Switzerland, www.hiking-in-switzerland.ch.

Information via your mobile telephone

Mobile Tagging with BeeTaggs provides you with information via your mobile phone. Using the camera on your mobile phone, you scan the BeeTagg code and then call up service information on the various stages via Internet. In particular this includes the latest information on accommodation, which you can also locate on a small map. The cost of the service depends upon your provider's tariff for data transfer.

To use this service you need a mobile phone with a camera (list of compatible phones at www.beetagg.com) and the free BeeTagg-Reader.

If the BeeTagg-Reader is not already available on your mobile phone, you need only install it once. This is fast and easy:

Step 1: send an SMS with the text «bee» to 989 or surf with your mobile phone to http://get.beetagg.com

Step 2: follow the instructions to install the BeeTagg Reader

Step 3: start the BeeTagg Reader and scan in the required BeeTagg with the camera

The route information panels are green for hikers, light blue for cyclists, ochre for mountain bikers and violet for skaters. These colours are also used to illustrate the routes e.g. on information signs and Internet.
If signs are missing or damaged, please use our feedback form at www.hiking-in-switzerland.ch.

Please note: no claim to increased liability can be assumed from red and yellow signs.

SwitzerlandMobility signposts

The signposts in Switzerland are classified by colour: red, depending on the Mobility pictogram stands for cycling, mountain biking and skating routes, and yellow for hiking.
SwitzerlandMobility routes are shown on the signposts in a uniform system of route information panels identified by numbers.
One-digit numbers stand for national routes, two-digit numbers for regional routes.

Up into the mountains!

50 round tours of different lengths and degrees of difficulty in all areas of the Swiss Alps and Jura. Each with detailed information, map extract and numerous photographs.

David Coulin
Die schönsten Rundwanderungen in den Schweizer Alpen
128 pages, 180 colour photos, 50 map extracts
Fr. 46.–

Für Gutes, das von oben kommt.

In unseren Bergen hergestellte Produkte.
Und bei jedem Kauf geht ein fixer Betrag an die Coop
Patenschaft für Berggebiete. So helfen Sie, die Zukunft
der Berge und Bergbevölkerung zu sichern.
Pro Montagna. Für unsere Berge. Für unsere Bauern.

Für mich und dich.

General signalization of Switzerland's hiking-route network

 Hiking trails generally lead aside from roads with motorized traffic and are usually not surfaced with asphalt or concrete. They do not make any special demands upon users.

 Yellow signposts provide information on location, hiking destinations and hiking time (excluding stops).

 Yellow rhombuses confirm the route of the hiking trail. Yellow directional arrows clarify which direction to take.

 Mountain trails access partially difficult terrain and are mostly steep, narrow and exposed in places. Users must be surefooted, have a head for heights, be physically fit and have mountain experience. Solid boots, equipment suited to the weather conditions and a topographical map are essential.

 Yellow signposts with white-red-white tips provide information on location, hiking destinations and hiking time (excluding stops).

  White-red-white painted stripes confirm the route of the hiking trail. White-red-white directional arrows clarify which direction to take.

 Alpine routes are challenging mountain trails leading partially across glaciers and through rocks with short climbing sections. It should not be assumed that any structural precautions have been provided. Users must be surefooted, have a head for heights and be extremely fit. Alpine experience and appropriate equipment are essential.

 Blue signposts with white-blue-white tip provide information on location, hiking destinations and hiking time (excluding stops).

 White-blue-white painted stripes confirm the route of the Alpine trail. White-blue-white directional arrows clarify which direction to take.

 The information panels at the beginning of Alpine routes indicate special requirements.

Additional signalization of hiking routes in «Hiking in Switzerland»

These routes meet demands for high quality (quality objectives of Hiking in Switzerland). The standard of quality is considerably higher than for the remainder of the hiking trail network.

International long-distance routes, are as far as possible, part of the national routes of Hiking in Switzerland. Where international long-distance routes lead along national routes, the route information panel is supplemented by a blue corner.

National routes cross through a large part of Switzerland and their starting points and destinations are usually close to the border. They are signposted with a route information panel and a one-digit number.

Regional routes lead through several cantons and are signposted with a route information panel and a two-digit number.

Local routes are particularly attractive hiking trails and are signposted with an information panel and a name or logo.

In Switzerland, hiking and mountain biking routes are sometimes signposted together. Mutual consideration is an essential requirement for shared use of the trails.

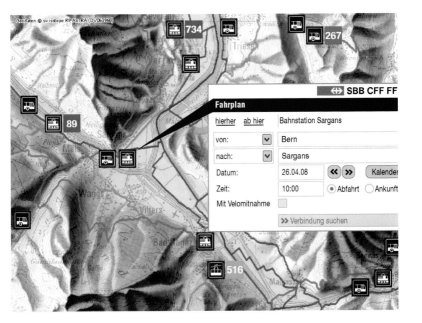

Rail, bus boat

The public transport system supplies Hiking in Switzerland with a regular timetable. Make use of these advantages:

1. To travel to the departure point and back home
2. To shorten a long one-day stage or because of rain
3. For variety, e.g. combining a hike with a boat cruise
4. To negotiate greater height differences
5. To bypass less attractive sections

On points 3 to 5, SwitzerlandMobility has prepared and numbered suggestions for use of public transport.

In Hiking in Switzerland, these numbers are on a green background and combined with the corresponding symbol for the means of transport, such as a symbol of a postbus.

You will find these symbols under the route descriptions of the stages in this route guide. All related timetables and reservation numbers are found at www.hiking-in-switzerland.ch .ch (see adjacent illustration).

The hiking times given in this book were calculated with the aid of a Geographic Information System (GIS). Thanks to the basic data, these are likely to be on the generous side.

Via Alpina: variety on the mountain and in the valley

The Via Alpina crosses 14 of Switzerland's most beautiful (pre-)Alpine passes and is classed as medium difficulty. Hikers experience an overwhelming diversity of culture, geology and topography across six Swiss cantons. Tranquil oases of relaxation alternate with thriving tourism centres. Wide roads end in dizzyingly high ridge trails. In addition, there is a unique opportunity to get to know Swiss Alpine culture in all its facets. Ultra-modern alps with pipelines and a showroom are just as much a feature on the trail as are alp huts where pigs, goats and cows watch an Alpine herdsman making cheese in a copper cauldron over an open fire. The scene changes from a pleasant family holiday resort to sophisticated perfume miles on expensive boulevards. The route is lined with the world's most singular diversity of flora and fauna. Shifts and thrust faults, depressions and rockfalls are an indication of our country's eventful geological history. Breathtaking panoramas alternate with tiny wayside gems and those who have worked up an appetite will find many gastronomic treats in store.

For many of the people in Canton Bern, Switzerland ends at Winterthur: to them, Eastern Switzerland is «terra incognita», and Switzerland's true endpoint – according to a song by Swiss songwriter Mani Matter – is Rorschach. The people of Eastern Switzerland naturally see things rather differently. After all, they represent six cantons (St. Gallen, Thurgau, Schaffhausen, Glarus, Appenzell Ausserrhoden and Innerrhoden) as well as the Principality of Liechtenstein as an «associated district». Eastern Switzerland is justly proud of its healthy economy but often feels discriminated against by the federal administration in Bern. Is this down to the distance from the capital city?

In fact Eastern Switzerland has far more to offer than merely Olma bratwürste (sausages) and a distinctive dialect. First and foremost, a lush green landscape with the Alpstein enthroned in the centre. If you turn a circle on the Säntis summit, to the north you see the hills of the Appenzell region flattening out and shimmering Lake Constance, to the west the Mittelland wrapped in haze, to the south rows of mountains

with snow-capped summits on the horizon and to the east, the Rhine Valley – in fact the whole of Eastern Switzerland. The landscape is simply made for hiking. Experienced mountain hikers will find countless trails leading through the Alpstein massif, to the seven Churfirsten and to the high peaks of the Glarus Alps. Moderately experienced hikers will find any number of hiking paths through the meadows and forests of the Appenzell and St. Gallen regions. Those simply seeking a pleasant stroll will find numerous paths through the fruit gardens of Thurgau and to the Rhine Falls at Schaffhausen.

Eastern Switzerland also comes up trumps in a cultural sense, beginning with the city of St. Gallen, where the Abbey District is a Unesco World Heritage and the Abbey Library enjoys international acclaim, to baroque monasteries, fortresses, medieval towns and impressive castles, the most famous of which is the castle of Vaduz. But the artistically painted houses in the Appenzell region, traditional folk music, ancient customs such as the Silvesterkläuse parade (mummers) in Urnäsch, colourful cattle drives to and from the alp and carefully cultivated folk music are equally as much part of Eastern Switzerland's vibrant cultural scene.

Pearls of the Rhine Valley

One of the loveliest hiking routes in the Alpine chain begins in the appealing Principality of Liechtenstein, on sun-kissed Alp Gaflei under the craggy Drei Schwestern summits, which tower above Vaduz and offer a remarkable ridge hike. Below Gaflei, a 15-metre-high stone vantage tower opens up views of the Rhine Valley and the Swiss Alvier group. In a forest clearing 400 metres above Vaduz, you come upon the Wild-schloss (Schalun Castle ruins), built at the end of the 12th century and used into the 14th century. On the west side, a barbecue spot lets you savour a grilled kebab while admiring the views.

The famous castle of the Prince of Liechtenstein towers majestically over the capital Vaduz, a town which has much to offer in the way of cultural, artistic and culinary attractions. The sunny, calciferous slopes in «Ländle» (the local name for Liechenstein) produce fine wines. The Rhine is crossed both custom-free and carefree over the covered wooden bridge at Sevelen.

The moist, shady slopes make hiking easier in the Werdenberg region and provide ideal

The Rhine Valley at Sargans

conditions for profuse numbers of mushrooms and toadstools to shoot up. With enough time in reserve, it's well worth exploring the gorge trail through the Geissberg ravine. The Wartauer Sagenweg (Fables Trail) introduces you to ancient spine-chillers and also adds variety.

The Restaurant Bergwerk in an old gallery entrance of the iron mine at Gonzen near Sargans gives a glimpse into the tough

times of mining in our country. In Sargans, the castle with its museum and the old town are interesting places to visit.

Vaduz Castle

Vaduz (Gaflei)		0:00	🚐 388 ❄	7 h 55 min	🕐
Wildschloss	1:35	1:35	🔥🏠	26,0 km	↔
Vaduz	1:20	2:55	🚐🍴🛏🏨🏠	620 m	↗
Sevelen	1:15	4:10	🚐🍴🛏🏨	1735 m	↘
Azmoos	1:45	5:55	🚐🍴🛏	high	🚶
Sargans	2:00	7:55	🚆🚐🍴🛏🏨❄🏠	238 T Montafon,	🏙
				237 T Walenstadt	

In Canton St. Gallen's longest valley

Commercially prosperous Mels with its many shopping centres has kept its intact, quaint village centre. The municipal district covers 139 square kilometres, extends to the Pizol and is 125-times larger than the municipality of Sargans. Fitness is now in demand for the first ascent to the tiny mountain hamlet of Vermol. Up here, views sweep from the Falknis to the Gonzen and for the first time into the lengthy valley of Weisstannental. Only ten minutes to the west, Lake Chapfen is an inseparable part of Vermol and rewards the detour with a colourful moorland landscape that will send all nature lovers into raptures.

The Weisstannental Valley was discovered and settled as far back as the days of the Walsers. The high-level trail on the western slope rewards you with sweeping views into St. Gallen's longest valley. Tiny Schwendi has a guest house. The surrounding mountain ridges are reflected in its idyllic trout pond. The shady spruce forest on the valley floor ensures that hikers do not work up too much of a sweat and the murmuring Seez provides another cool down. Here the trail scarcely touches the road.

The small silver fir is enjoying a revival. The old sawmill at the side of the village stream cuts the trees into planks for the building in-

dustry and cows are driven through pleasant farming villages. Hikers will find a comfortable place to stay overnight at the Hotel Gemse. Time seems to pass at a more leisurely pace in such serene seclusion.

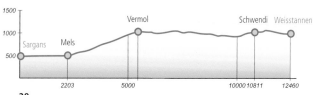

Mels

Weisstannen

Sargans		0:00	🚂🚌 201 ✕ 🏂 🎠 ☀ 🏰	4 h 50 min	🕐
Mels	0:35	0:35	🚌✕🏂🛏🌳	12,5 km	↔
Vermol	1:45	2:20	🏂☀	940 m	↗
Schwendi	2:00	4:20	🚌✕🏂	440 m	↘
Weisstannen	0:30	4:50	🚌✕🏂	medium	🚶
				237 T Walenstadt	🗺

29

Waterfalls and modern alps

Alp Siez is considered one of the most modern alps in Switzerland. Milk is delivered from milking parlours on the surrounding alps by pipeline and processed in a show dairy fitted with the latest equipment. The wide range of products is sold throughout Switzerland.

On the Falinenstock on the eastern side of the valley, you can savour bread, cheese and milk while watching Switzerland's third-highest waterfall in its vertical plunge to the valley. The new trail section over a steep rockslide area is not recommended in heavy rain. Views sweep over the vertical and narrowest rock step in the valley to the rear

Alp Mittlere Stafel

Foo Pass with views into the Glarus region

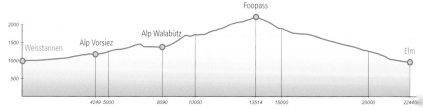

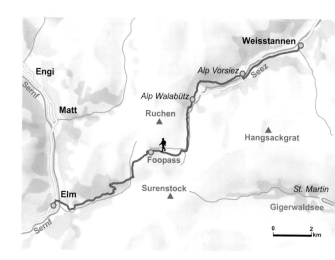

Weisstannen Valley. Increasing amounts of black slate in this area are a reminder of the proximity of the mountains of Glarus.

On Alp Foo you find one of the last drinking troughs before tackling the steep pass into the Glarus region. A wide horizon opens up from this first pass on the Via Alpina, with the Hausstock, Selbsanft and Tödi lined up in a row. On Raminer Alp, farm buildings are offset one above the other like a string of pearls and a glance into the simple buildings reveals a modern, tiled dairy.

After the downhill section over the Mittleren Stafel and the new wooden bridge, hikers

rapidly lose height and plunge into the characteristic, deeply furrowed valleys at the foot of the Glarus Vorab. In addition to the Suvorov House, Elm has a number of other impressive historic buildings in its village centre, including a former slate factory, now a museum with the past illustrated on panels.

Weisstannen		0:00	🚐 ✕ 🛏	8 h 55 min	🕐
Alp Vorsiez	1:20	1:20	🚐 ✕ 🛏 🏪	22,4 km	↔
Alp Walabütz	1:25	2:45	✕ 🌳	1505 m	↗
Foopass	3:05	5:50	❄	1530 m	↘
Elm	3:05	8:55	🚐 🏛 ✕ 🛏 🏪 🏠 🌳	high	🚶
				247 T Sardona	🏞

Breezy ridges and bright flora

Langstaffel in Durnachtal

Richetli Pass

Amongst other things, Elm is famous for its Martinsloch: a hole in the rock of the Tchingelhörner, through which the rays of the sun shine on the Elm church tower just four times every year. The lovely village lies in the centre of the Geopark, with its fascinating geological rock thrust line on the mountain border to the Graubunden and St. Gallen regions. This main thrust fault has been nominated as a potential Unesco World Heritage. The trail climbs easily through a varied agricultural area to sun-kissed Ampächli, which can also be reached by aerial cableway. The high-level trail to Erbsalp offers the chance to study the Glarus thrust sheet on the Tschingelhörner.

Hikers should take care to ration both drinks and stamina in the heat of the southern slope of the mighty Kärpf as there are no further refreshment chances for hours. But as compensation, the sunny slope offers a vast variety of flora and fauna. Arnica, lobelia and edelweiss edge the trail to the Erbser Stock with its impressive ridge approach. Here the horizon widens out, with views to Wichlenalp with the silted-up Lake Wichel and to the Richetli Pass. The colourful

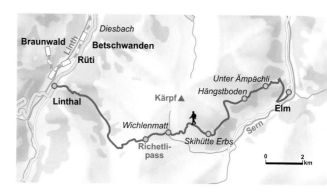

high moorland encircled by rugged summits resembles a giant amphitheatre. During the final uphill section on crumbling slate, it becomes clear why this pass is not recommended in wet weather. Dry conditions are also essential for the descent along a narrow path over steep, exposed grass slopes into the Durnach Valley.

Alp Wichelmatt

Elm		0:00	🚌🚡202🍴🛏️🏪🎒🏞️	10 h 20 min	🕐
Unter Ämpächli	2:05	2:05	🏡🍴🛏️	24,3 km	↔️
Hängstboden	0:40	2:45	🍹	1745 m	↗️
Skihütte Erbs	1:20	4:05	🚌🍴🛏️	2055 m	↘️
Wichlenmatt	1:55	6:00	🏞️	high	🚶
Richetlipass	0:40	6:40	❄️	247 T Sardona, 246 T Klausenpass	🗺️
Linthal	3:40	10:20	🚂🚌🍴🛏️🏪		

From a sunny terrace to Switzerland's largest alp

Linthal sits in the middle of Switzerland's deepest valley, known as the Glarus «Zigerschlitzes». Here, between rugged walls and striking mountains, use is made of the force of the water thundering down from the heights. In the shade of trees on the west side of the valley, hikers reach the sun terrace of Braunwald, a centre of soft family, senior and sport tourism. Three challenging fixed-rope routes have been installed for the more sporty. A road above extensive bands of rock leads hikers, bikers and horse-drawn carriages to the Nussbühl panorama restaurant. The mountain of cream on your

Horse-drawn carriage in Braunwald

coffee and the mountains on the horizon ensure a sunny mood.

Urnerboden begins with an area of moorland on the southern side of the valley alongside the waters of the Fätschbach. In summer, the largest Swiss alp in Switzerland, which belongs to the municipality of Spiringen, can graze up to 1200 cows. The green Alpine pastures stretch a full 13 kilometres into Canton Glarus. The Walker fa-

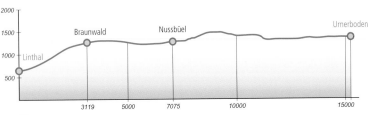

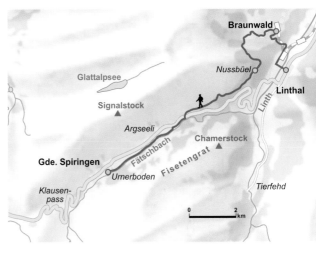

Urnerboden

mily are trying to keep this beautiful corner of the world alive in winter, but as the Klausen Pass is closed in winter, all supplies must be brought from the Glarus side. Thus the Urnerboden population – still numbering 40 – is pure Urner in summer with a few from Glarus in winter.

The Fiseten ridge has become a popular excursion destination, quickly to reached by aerial cableway. The glaciers of the Gemsfairenstock, Clariden and Tödi spread out before you and you may spot a plane landing far below on the Hüfi Glacier.

Linthal		0:00	🚂🚌 205 🚡 203 ✕ 🛏 🛒	5 h 55 min	🕐
Braunwald	2:00	2:00	🚡 ✕ 🛏 🛒	15,2 km	↔
Nussbüel	1:10	3:10	✕	1180 m	↗
Urnerboden	2:45	5:55	🚌 ✕ 🛏	465 m	↘
				high	🚶
				246 T Klausenpass	🏔

The heart of Switzerland was long ruled by fierce warriors, who defended the lovely landscape around the Urnersee lake with great pride. Even today, hikers can still find traces of the time of Switzerland's birth at many world-famous historic sites. The men under the flag of the Uristiers were considered extremely fierce fighters and laid claim to the Alps from deep into the Glarus region with Urnerboden to as far as Engelberg. The people of Central Switzerland are still rather reserved towards strangers and foreigners, hence international tourism has only really developed between Lucerne and Engelberg, with its glaciated Titlis and famous revolving aerial gondola.

Göschenen and Andermatt experienced the first heyday of tourism with the opening of the Gotthard Pass and its crossing by Gotthard postal coach. Since modern times, the villages are often bypassed on the motorway as a mere scenic backdrop. Happily, foreign investment is helping Andermatt to new prosperity.

With its many lakes nestling in a rolling hill and mountain landscape and easily accessible scenic summits, Central Switzerland is rated as one of the most beautiful regions in the world. Hikers will find hundreds of different routes, from paths suitable for a baby buggy to dizzying ridge trails. The remote valley of Maderanertal with Lake Golzern and the Göscheneralp Valley, where the setting of the Dammastock over dark-green Lake Göscheneralp will leave you lost for words, are considered ultimate highlights. In such remote valleys, older mountain farmers still keep up the tradition of Wildheuet, meaning cutting grass on frighteningly steep slopes using long scythes.

The huts of the Swiss Alpine Club offer excellent hospitality and shorten the route to glaciated and remote three-thousand-metre peaks. Postbuses carry visitors up to major Alpine passes, where lovely high-level trails lead past traditional alps. In the heart of Switzerland, hikers can look forward to friendly encounters in a traditional, unspoilt landscape.

Alpine tradition and a glacier world

Bee boxes are found at several spots along the uphill route to the Klausen Pass. Ten years ago, a bee breeder from Lucerne placed the industrious pollen gatherers in the middle of this wealth of flora as the bees in his fruit orchards were unable to take flight because of the nets used as protection against hailstorms.

Below the Klausen Pass, many small and simple Alpine huts still nestle in recesses in the rock, giving an interesting insight into the traditional way of life on the alp. This is where worn cheesecloths are still hung up to dry in the open air. The Klausen Pass has been accessible by car and motorbike since 1948 and is a very popular excursion destination with panoramic views of the Urner und Glarus mountain world. The Clariden, Schärhorn and Gross Windgällen peaks form an impressive backdrop high above the pass

Tell monument in Altdorf

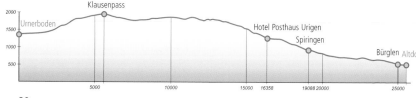

road that snakes up from Schächental. Below the picturesque Klausen Pass Hotel, several alps spread out high above the road on the southern flank of the Ruosalper Chulm. The Alps of Central Switzerland from the Krönten to the Uri-Rotstock mark the horizon on the descent to Spiringen. The village is as small as the municipal district is large. The district extends over the entire Urnerboden. The centre of Bürglen with its fortified tower has such a historic feel that you might expect William Tell to suddenly appear around a corner. The Tell Educational Trail to Altdorf illustrates the exploits of our national hero. The many impressive buildings bear witness to Altdorf's turbulent past.

Heidmanegg with Lägend Windgällen

On the Schächental high-level trail

Urnerboden		0:00	🚌 205 🍴 🏠	8 h 50 min	🕐
Klausenpass	2:25	2:25	🚌 204 🍴 🏠 ❄	25,5 km	↔
Hotel Posthaus Urigen	3:35	6:00	🚌 🍴 🏠	1090 m	↗
Spiringen	1:00	7:00	🚌 🍴 🏠 🏪	1930 m	↘
Bürglen (UR)	1:40	8:40	🚌 🍴 🏠 🏪 🏛	high	🚶
Altdorf	0:10	8:50	🚂 🚌 🍴 🏠 🏪 🏛	246 T Klausenpass	🏔

39

Natural history flights of fancy

Alp Uf der Lauwi with Titlis

Brüsti with Brunnistock

Kayakers often ride the wild waves of the Schächen river at Attinghausen. From here the trail climbs partly between natural-stone walls up to the Brusti summit station, a varied area of protected flora and moorland. The high-level natural history trail swings in bold steps over the Chraienhöreli ridge and the Geissrücken. The Surenen Pass is considered one of the most popular passes in Central Switzerland.

The mighty Brunnistock frequently hurls stones and avalanches down from its jagged cliffs on to the hiking trail below the Surenen Pass. It is advisable to avoid its south flank in a wide arch and to keep an eye on the mountain, especially in thunderstorms and the spring snow that can lay here for a long time.

As early as medieval times, the Urners crossed the Surenen Pass to pillage and plunder, advancing as far as the Engelberg Monastery. No one was able to stop the fierce warriors and so they were given the alp rights up as far as Alpenrösli near Engelberg. This is why the black bull on the yellow flag still greets hikers far into the Engelberg Valley.

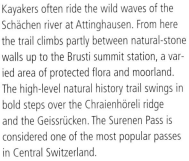

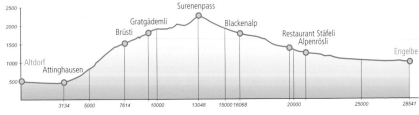

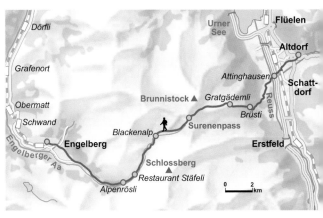

Dörfli · Flüelen · Altdorf · Grafenort · Urner See · Attinghausen · Schatt-dorf · Obermatt · Brunnistock ▲ · Gratgädemli · Brüsti · Schwand · Blackenalp · Surenenpass · Engelberg · Erstfeld · Engelberger Aa · Schlossberg ▲ · Restaurant Stäfeli · Alpenrösli · 0 2 km

On Blackenalp you can enjoy refreshments or light a candle in the chapel, awed by the large valley basin encircled by mighty bastions of rock.

Canton Obwalden begins at the Restaurant Alpenrösli with the municipal district of Engelberg. A shady road leads past the Fürenalp railway station and through the long valley to Engelberg. Milk from the alp is made into the famous monastery cheese in a monastery show dairy.

Chraienhöreli

Altdorf		0:00			11 h 30 min
Attinghausen	0:45	0:45			28,5 km
Brüsti	3:15	4:00			2080 m
Gratgädemli	1:00	5:00			1595 m
Surenenpass	2:05	7:05			high
Blackenalp	1:05	8:10			246 T Klausenpass, 245 T Stans
Restaurant Stäfeli	1:05	9:15			
Alpenrösli	0:20	9:35			
Engelberg	1:55	11:30			

To the loveliest pre-Alpine mountain lake

Hotel names such as the «Europäischer Hof» are evidence of international tourism in the monastery village of Engelberg, on sunny days a meeting place for the entire world. Everyone throngs to the Titlis aerial cableway, where the cabin turns once on its own axis as it glides up over the glacier. Once on the Titlis, excited tourists can even hold a snowball fight in mid-summer. Hikers can find the quieter corners on the path to the Trubsee lake, a little away from the cableway. After Restaurant Gerschnialp, the path soon winds around steep, over-grown bends up to the Trübsee cableway station. Marmots in an enclosure can be ad-mired at close quarters and many Alpine plants are illustrated on small panels. If the Trübsee lake had not existed, the people of Engelberg would have had to invent it: hikers make the most of its attractive shores and its waters reflect the surrounding mountain world.

Canton Bern with Engstlenalp spreads out to the west of the Joch Pass. The Engstlen-see, one of the largest mountain lakes in Canton Bern, nestles dark blue in a rugged limestone landscape. A unique variety of

Alpine flora and thousands of Alpine roses thrive on sunny slopes.

Thanks to gentle renovation, the Hotel Engstlenalp has been able to preserve its 19th century charm to the present day. A perfect spot to stay overnight and wallow in nostalgia. Tank up on energy at a natural hotspot between the hotel and lake. Anyone suffering from stress can unwind by watch-ing the calm fishermen on the lake shores.

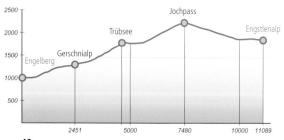

Engstlensee

On the Joch pass

Engelberg		0:00	🚐🚃🚡207✕🍴🛒	5 h 25 min	🕐
Gerschnialp	1:10	1:10	🚡✕🍴	11,1 km	↔
Trübsee	1:25	2:35	🚡208✕🍴	1285 m	↗
Jochpass	1:45	4:20	🚡208✕🍴❄	455 m	↘
Engstlenalp	1:05	5:25	🚐✕🍴🏠	high	🚶
				245 T Stans, 255 T Sustenpass	🗺

43

The Bernese Oberland became world famous through its main attractions, the Eiger, Mönch & Jungfrau, with their impressive, glaciated northern flanks. The mountains helped the Oberland to gain the best touristic infrastructure in Switzerland, including the pioneering development of the Jungfraujoch into Europe's highest-altitude railway station. But despite this, the cosmopolitan centres of Grindelwald and Gstaad have been able to preserve their charisma with many chalets bearing wonderful wood carvings.

From the two central lakes of Thun and Brienz with their historic castles, many different valleys branch off towards the south as far as the highest mountains. The change from the rolling landscape of the Simmen Valley to the steep, high flanks of the Lauterbrunnen Valley offers hikers an incomparable diversity of landscape in a very compact area. You share the natural scenic beauty with thousands of tourists on Kleine Scheidegg – and with chamois on the Grossen Lohner. In Gstaad the entire world meets along the perfume mile, whilst the

Adelboden cableways are usually shared
with Swiss families.
In the Oberland, several of Switzerland's
highest waterfalls cascade over steep cliffs
whilst in the Alpine foothills, the water
keeps the moorland moist. Many rocky passes take hikers close to an impressive glacier
world and into conversation with mountain-
eers in famous huts. It's amazing how
many alps have been able to retain their
traditional values despite their proximity
to tourist centres.
The Bernese Oberland offers so many excursion and hiking attractions that one lifetime
is barely sufficient. There is also a vast variety of culinary and cultural options. The
choice ranges from beach volleyball tournaments to yodelling festivals. The easy-going,
dry-humoured but open-hearted character
of the Bernese Oberland people makes
possible many enriching encounters. A hike
in the Oberland offers adventure, variety
and pure recreation.

Hiking heaven

Before the well-secured trail clambers up along the walls of the Spycherflue to Tannalp, it's worth taking a look at the special Alpine flora on the steep grass slopes. Tannalp is an ensemble of Alpine dairy, mountain guest house and chapel. The Tannalp Lake turns this area leading from Melchsee-Frutt into a dream destination for hikers. The highlight of this one-day stage is the ridge of the Erzegg via Balmeregg to Planplatten – a hike near to heaven with the Wetterhorn, Mittelhorn and Rosenhorn in your sights. The glaciated Trift area opens out to the south.

The Alpentower of the Meiringen-Hasliberg Aerial Cableway stands at Planplatten. And not without reason, for the views from here to Lake Brienz and Meiringen are simply breathtaking. These fantastic views never leave you as you descend the narrow trail down the mountain ridge. Alp Oberegg offers culinary delights with dairy produce. The trail then wends its way through the forest along the Muggenstutz to Reuti. The Muggenstutz Hasli Dwarf shows how to market a region successfully: most children are

familiar with this dwarf from four children's books, CDs and cassettes.

Adults will find a sculpture garden with annually-changing exhibitions at Schrändli on the steep descent to Meiringen. Meringue, the popular dessert made from sugar and whipped egg whites, owes its name to

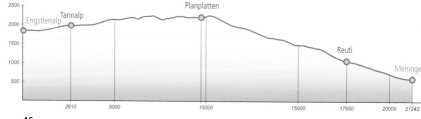

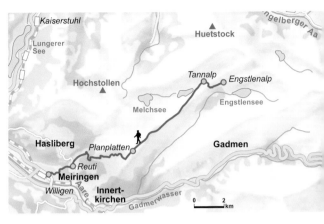

Erzegggrat with Wetterhorn group

Hotel Engstlenalp

Meiringen where it was invented. The town is set in the midst of wild waters and with the Aareschlucht gorge and Reichenbach Falls, already fascinated travellers in bygone days.

Engstlenalp		0:00	🚠 ✗ 🛏 🏠 🌳	7 h 55 min	🕐
Tannalp	0:55	0:55	✗ 🛏	21,2 km	↔
Planplatten	2:55	3:50	🚡 209 ✗ ❋	890 m	↗
Reuti	2:55	6:45	🚡 ✗ 🛏	2120 m	↘
Meiringen	1:10	7:55	🚉 🚌 🚡 ✗ 🛏 🏭 🌳	high	🚶
				255 T Sustenpass	🗺

47

Cascading water and impressive peaks

View towards Eiger

Gross Scheidegg

The first highlight of the climb is reached early on. It is thanks to the pioneering spirit of our forefathers that today, from the dizzying height of a small platform, we can experience the immense mass of water at the Reichenbach Falls thundering into the depths. The forbidding cliffs above the trail are also saturated and covered in glistening moss.

The Zwirgi guest house perches on a rise on the cliffs above the falls, affording one of the most beautiful views down to Meiringen. The trail leads through the Reichenbach Valley in shady forest, to reach the wide valley floor and the frequently photographed views of the Wetterhorn and Engelhorn peaks.

You would expect to see horse-drawn coaches rather than a collection of cars at the nostalgic Rosenlaui Hotel. This splendid building still has an air of the pioneering spirit of the time and early Alpine tourism. Totally awestruck you move through the romantic halls and creaking bedchambers without running water, where Tolstoi, Nietzsche and Goethe once trod. The Rosenlaui glacier gorge, where the glacier melt

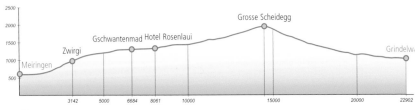

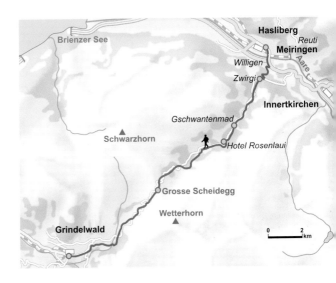

forces its way through 80-metre-high rock walls, is considered a natural monument of national importance.

From Schwarzwaldalp on, the trees become wilder and sparser and the colourful moorland on Chalberboden ever more extensive. Goats and calves discover their reflections in various small ponds. Grosse Scheidegg rates as a personal challenge for many racing cyclists and bikers as well as an experience highlight.

Oberland idyll

Meiringen		0:00	🚌 210 🍴 ⛺ 🏨 🌳	8 h 30 min	🕐
Zwirgi	1:30	1:30	🚌 🍴 ⛺ ❄	22,9 km	↔
Gschwantenmad	1:25	2:55	🌲	1530 m	↗
Hotel Rosenlaui	0:20	3:15	🚌 🍴 ⛺ 🏨	1095 m	↘
Grosse Scheidegg	2:35	5:50	🚌 211 🍴 ⛺ ❄	high	🚶
Grindelwald	2:40	8:30	🚈 🚌 🍴 ⛺ 🏨	255 T Sustenpass,	🏛
				254 T Interlaken	

Hiking beneath a world-famous backdrop

Asians have long known where the world is at its most beautiful. The Wetterhorn, Schreckhorn, Eiger – a phenomenal open-air stage set dominates Grindelwald. The traditional, timber chalet building style is still cultivated here and now and again along vanity mile you'll also spot a farmer with a loaded hay cart. A wide «Grüezi» (greetings) trail leads over Kleine Scheidegg. Encounters with other hikers are a regular event here and all greet each other eagerly in a host of different languages.

Brandegg offers beautiful panoramic views together with food and drink. Railway fans are given plenty of opportunity to photograph the nostalgic Jungfrau Railway trains. Kleine (small) Scheidegg, which is actually higher than Grosse (great) Scheidegg, welcomes travellers and adventurers from all over the world. The dark-brown timber-built hotels are evidence of an age-old tradition. Goats cavort at the railway station providing a subject for tourist cameras. Here the world-famous backdrop of the Eiger, Mönch

Uphill at Wärgistal

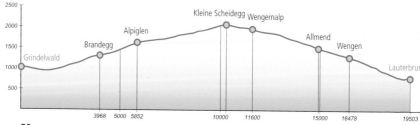

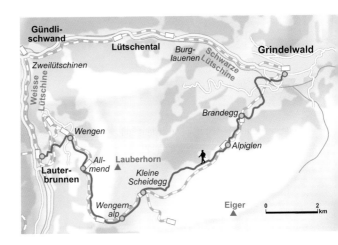

Kleine Scheidegg

& Jungfrau towers directly before you. It's impossible for expert climbers to move one foothold on the sheer Eiger North Face

without being watched. It goes without saying that this world-famous spot must be shared with a multitude of other sightseers. Wengen, renowned for the Lauberhorn Ski Races, has plenty of laid-back leisure to offer in summer. Many classic hotel buildings and chalets blend harmoniously into sunny hollows on the mountain slopes. The steep winding forest trail down to Lauterbrunnen and the famous Staubbach Falls is conquered in the opposite direction by Jungfrau Marathon runners, always more or less on their limit.

Grindelwald		0:00		7 h 25 min
Brandegg	1:35	1:35		19,5 km
Alpiglen	0:55	2:30		1230 m
Kleine Scheidegg	1:50	4:20		1465 m
Wengernalp	0:20	4:40		high
Allmend	1:05	5:45		254 T Interlaken
Wengen	0:25	6:10		
Lauterbrunnen	1:15	7:25		

On the trail of James Bond

The root-strewn path from Lauterbrunnen to Mürren demands a certain level of fitness but the steep mountain slopes have to be mastered somehow. All your effort is rewarded on the high terraces of traffic-free Mürren with fabulous views towards the Eiger, Mönch & Jungfrau. Mürren and the Schilthorn became world-famous through the James Bond film «On Her Majesty's Secret Service» but Wengen has remained the dream destination of the rich and beautiful. Mürren, the highest-altitude inhabited village in Canton Bern, offers more out-of-the-way alps and less-used hiking trails. The former Walser settlement is still recognizable by the building style of the older houses.

In its simplicity, Spielbodenalp seems detached from the world-famous region. Freshly fortified, the hiker can take in his stride the steep ramp up to Bryndli with its varied and colourful flora. The wide valley to the Rotstock Hut lies in the shadows of the Gspaltenhorn, Bütlasse and Schilthorn peaks.

The sturdy Rotstock Hut breaks up the long ascent to the Sefinenfurgge. This pass into the rear Kiental Valley gets appreciably steeper and demands sure-footedness along the narrow trail. It's worth climbing from the Sefinenfurgge to a natural vantage platform with overwhelming views of the Blüemlisalp. Wooden stairways and fixed ropes help to master the steep gulley on the north-west side. A fascinating waterfall cascades over the forbidding cliff barrier at Oberen Dürrenberg. Alp Bürgli provides visitors with goats' milk and other dairy products.

Lauterbrunnen

Drättehorn ▲

Winteregg

Sand-
bach

Schilthorn ▲

Mürren

Weisse Lütschine

Spielbodenalp

Stechel-
berg

Griesalp

Alp Bürgli

Rotstockhütte

Gimmelwald

Sefinenfurgge

0   2
              km

Ascent to the Sefinenfurgge

Guests can choose from three mountain inns at Griesalp: the Golderli with a Himalayan atmosphere, the Naturfreundehaus with its special wood-burning oven in the kitchen and the Berghaus Griesalp with its large dining room.

Sefinenfurgge

Lauterbrunnen		0:00	🚌🚐🚟216✖🛏🏪🌲	10 h	🕐
Mürren	3:15	3:15	🏠🛏✖🛏🏪	20,5 km	↔
Spielbodenalp	0:55	4:10	✖🛏	2090 m	↗
Rotstockhütte	1:30	5:40	✖🛏🌲	1495 m	↘
Sefinenfurgge	1:50	7:30	❄	high	🚶
Alp Bürgli	1:45	9:15	✖	254 T Interlaken, 264 T Jungfrau	🗺
Griesalp	0:45	10:00	🚐🛏✖🛏		

Please note: long stage, see accommodation possibilities in Mürren, www.muerren.ch and at the Rotstockhut, www.rotstockhuette.ch.

53

So close to the glacier ...

Blümlisalp hut

Oeschinensee

The educational nature trail leading up through the forest from Griesalp provides information on local flora and then reaches the Obere Bundalp, where it's advisable to check your water reserves again because the coming ascent may be a hot one. The trail now leading along steep mountain slopes is often busy with hikers. In summer it's best to climb the 1000 metres height from here to Hohtürli early in the morning, unless you want to experience the human dramas that take place here on this baking-hot ascent at around 2 o'clock in the afternoon. The final phase of the climb to Hohtürli, at 2778 metres the highest point on the Via Alpina, is made easier by a wooden stair-way. The additional 50 metres up to the imposing Blüemlisalp Hut is well worth it. Here you can drink beer or tea with climbers who have scaled the ice-clad Blüemlisalp. The trail to the Oeschinen Lake loses height slowly so you can savour the sight of the Blüemlisalp, Fründenhorn and Doldenhorn mountains for a long time. There are several exposed but well-secured sections between

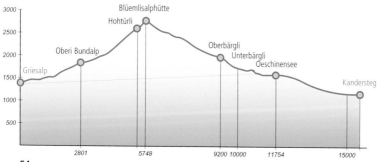

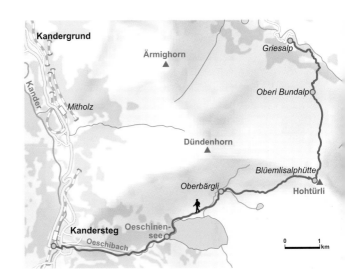

the mountain restaurants at Oberbärgli and Underbärgli. The Oeschinen Lake, one of the most beautiful of all mountain lakes, was created by a rockslide. The deep-blue lake, the waters of which are drunk in Kandersteg, nestles between craggy cliff faces. With its traditional wooden chalets, Kandersteg simply oozes Bernese Oberland charm.

Steps at Hohtürli

Griesalp		0:00	🚌🏠✕🛏	8 h 05 min	🕐
Oberi Bundalp	1:35	1:35	🏠✕🛏	15,6 km	↔
Hohtürli	2:30	4:05	❄	1545 m	↗
Blüemlisalphütte	0:10	4:05	✕🛏❄	1765 m	↘
Oberbärgli	1:35	5:50	✕🛏	high	🚶
Unterbärgli	1:35	5:50	✕🛏	264 T Jungfrau,	🗺
Oeschinensee	1:10	7:00	🏠214✕🛏	263 T Wildstrubel	
Kandersteg	1:05	8:05	🚠🚌✕🛏🛒		

Pleace note: long stage, see accommodation possibilities at the Blüemlisalp hut, www.bluemlisalphuette.com

On the lookout for chamois

You can warm up gently on the walk along the River Kander. After gaining some height, the trail climbs through the fascinating Alpbach gorge. The large Usser Üschene alp is bordered by the Lohner and Gällihorn peaks. The trail negotiates an exposed steep section with snaking bends to Alp Alpschele, where typical red-white Simmental cows gaze quizzically at the climbers. The cowherd's family always has drinks ready to offer guests.

The Lohner is home to several chamois colonies and you can easily make out these clever climbers among the loose rocks. Their movements loosen scores of stones and these can clearly be heard clattering down. Actually it's a wonder that the Lohner is still standing – it consists of loose, constantly crumbling layers of rock. A tower of rock at the top of the pass actually looks like a man-made cairn. The fascinating rock formations of the Bunderchrinde look as if they

Bunderchrinde

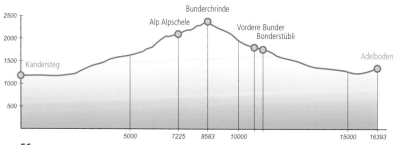

have had chunks bitten out of them. The sickle-like shape is clearly visible on the horizon and even seen from Adelboden. Meanwhile, the Oeschinen Lake glistens in the distance, in company with the Blüemlisalp, Fründenhorn and Doldenhorn peaks. To the southwest, the steeply-sloped Doldenhorn, Altels, Balmhorn and Rinderhorn reach skywards.

The Bonderalp mountain inn brings life to the high alp under the steep Lohner flanks and with other enterprises on the alp, keeps up the traditions of an Alpine dairy. Here the cheese is still made by hand in copper cauldrons and cheesecloths are hung out in the sun to dry.

Above: Kandersteg
Below: View of
Adelboden

Kandersteg		0:00	🚌🚐✖️🛏️🛒	7 h 30 min	🕐
Alp Alpschele	3:35	3:35	✖️	16,4 km	↔️
Bunderchrinde	0:55	4:30	❄️🌳	1430 m	↗️
Vordere Bunder	1:05	5:35	✖️	1260 m	↘️
Bonderstübli	0:10	5:45	✖️	high	🧍
Adelboden	1:45	7:30	🚌🚐✖️🛏️🛒	263 T Wildstrubel	🏨

A Mecca for model gliders

Adelboden, famous from the World Cup Ski Slalom on Chuenisbärgli, focuses on family tourism in summer. The elongated village on the south-east slopes of the Gsür has managed to preserve its traditional Bernese Oberland village character with wooden chalets. On an easy village stroll, you can enjoy flower-bedecked balconies, original decorations and hand-carved motifs; traditions that have been cultivated here for decades. And perhaps smile at the Place of Fame with its cement footprints of the ski aces who have won in Adelboden.

Many small moorland areas, rich in flora, line the path alongside the foaming Engstlige, through the valley of the same name, up to Geils. Here the forest becomes sparser; the moorland landscape spreads across the large, open hollow to the Hahnenmoospass. At Geilsbrüggli, the departure point of the Hahnenmoos aerial cableway, you'll find a group of rustic buildings where you can enjoy a break for refreshments.

In the 16th century, the Hahnenmoospass divided Protestant Adelboden from the Catholic Fribourg region. Today, thanks to good thermals, it's considered paradise for flying model gliders. On many weekends, pilots tinker feverishly in the old hotel and the surrounding area is occupied by aircraft. Six launching areas on the neighbouring hills allow aerial acrobatics in front of the beautiful backdrop of the Wildstrubel and the Plaine-Morte Glacier.

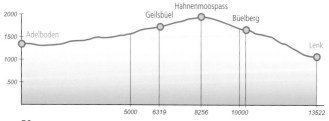

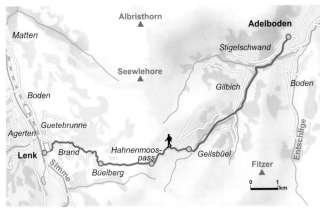

Büelberg

On the Lenk Valley side, the marshlands spread down to Restaurant Büelberg. From here you can enjoy views of the Fribourg Alps with Les Diablerets and the Wistätthorn, which towers above Lenk. The scattered settlements on the sunny slope add plenty of variety on the descent to Lenk.

On the Hahnenmoos Pass

Adelboden		0:00	🚌🚐215✕🛏🛒	5 h 10 min	🕐
Geilsbüel	2:20	2:20	🏔215✕	13,5 km	↔
Hahnenmoospass	0:55	3:15	🏔✕🛏❄	740 m	↗
Büelberg	0:40	3:55	✕🚐217	1020 m	↘
Lenk	1:15	5:10	🚌🚐✕🛏🛒	medium	🚶
				263 T Wildstrubel	🗺

In the realm of the lynx

Every child knows «Lenk Denk» (Lenk of course!) from Swiss TV adverts. The village, with its stately, multi-storeyed wooden houses, markets itself short, sharp and to the point. The buildings, adorned with woodcarvings and abundant floral decorations are wonderfully charismatic. With the Music Academy, Jazz Days, Transa-Summer Festival, cattle drives, hornussen tournaments, folklore festivals – there's entertainment in plenty as far as the farthest corner of the Simmen Valley.

The climb to the Wallegg mountain inn contains a few steps and offers plenty of

Learning about the lynx

variety as it leads through the dense ‹Wald am Bach› forest and past a near-to-nature pond. At the forest edge stands a row of busts of the five former directors of the Lenk Mountain Cableways, each beautifully carved in wood.

Easy-to-spot information panels point out that from here on you're in the realm of the lynx. It's worth taking a look inside the alp hut on the Oberen Lochbergalp. A simple inn with cheesemaking in a dark alcove with smoke extraction through the roof gable is a truly rare sight.

The Trüttlisberg Pass lies at the edge of a fascinating fissured limestone area with typical hollows and holes in the ground. Before setting off down to the Turbachtal Valley, it's worth spending time studying the phenomenal panoramic view, stretching from the Eiger to the Rochers de Naye.

The Turbachtal Valley is long and drawn out but refreshment is available at the Wintermatte-Beizli tavern. The Sunne-Stübli in Turbach offers traditional fare in rustic surroundings. The panorama trail above Gstaad affords views of chic chalets, with vistas of the Wildhorn and Les Diablerets worth millions.

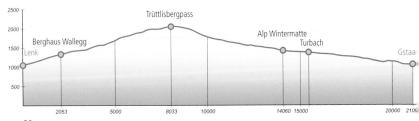

On the Trüttlisberg Pass

Wildstrubel from the Trüttlisberg Pass

Lenk		0:00	🚌🚐✕🏨🛒	7 h 10 min	🕐
Berghaus Wallegg	0:45	0:45	✕🏨	21,1 km	↔
Trüttlisbergpass	2:50	3:35	✳	1140 m	↗
Alp Wintermatte	1:45	5:20	✕	1150 m	↘
Turbach	0:40	6:00	✕🚐 365	high	🚶
Gstaad	1:50	7:10	🚌🚐✕🏨🛒	263 T Wildstrubel	🗺

Where worlds meet

The world and folklore meet in Gstaad. The perfume mile offers an unusual mix of Coco Chanel and biogas. Here, on the traffic free village square, the long-established farmer's wife encounters the lady of the world. Charming Gstaad is growing rapidly and there are ever more outrageously expensive wooden chalets. The events calendar resembles that of a city.

The trail climbs steeply up around winding curves alongside the Eggli aerial cableway (open in winter only). Calorie levels can be topped up again at the Eggli mountain guest house. A well-trodden path leads along the lengthy ridge with its sparse trees.

Eggli

The rocky Vanil Noir dominates the horizon to the north.

After lush alps you arrive at Wilde Bode (wild ground). This sandstone area is riddled with holes, exposed, and with wild vegetation certainly lives up to its name. This adventurous section is mastered with ladders and a very narrow little path.

The Col de Jable forms the language border to French-speaking Switzerland. Soon you reach the first alp and a building with a large shingle roof and a distinctive shingle-covered chimney. Everything here revolves around tradition. The L'Etivaz AOC, a full-fat

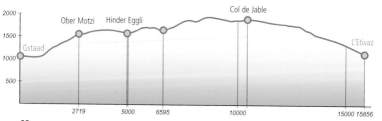

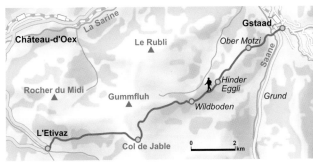

Alp Gros Jable

Les Salaires

hard cheese, is made in large copper cauldrons over an open fire by burly dairymen. Fellow dairymen on the other 125 alps around L'Etivaz produce 320 tonnes of cheese in the same way. After a steep descent you finally reach the small village that has become world famous for its cheese.

Gstaad		0:00	🚈🚌🚡218❌🏨🛒	4 h 25 min	🕐
Ober Motzi	0:35	0:35		15,9 km	↔
Hinder Eggli	0:10	0:45	❌❄	1250 m	↗
Wildboden	0:35	1:20		1165 m	↘
Col de Jable	1:15	2:35	❄	high	🚶
L'Etivaz	1:50	4:25	🚈🚌❌🛒	263 T Wildstrubel,	🏞
				262 T Rochers de Naye	

«We sat behind a rock protected from the wind, letting the sun shine upon us, the food and drink tasted wonderful. We watched the mist as it slowly dispersed, each of us discovered something, or thought he had discovered something. Gradually we saw Lausanne with all the summer houses around, Vevey and Chillon Castle quite clearly, the mountain that hid the entrance into the Valais, as far as the lake...» Johann Wolfgang von Goethe was enthralled by the views across Lake Geneva in 1779, when he climbed the summit of the Dôle during his travels in Switzerland.

The Lake Geneva area is a region of diverse landscapes. Lakes with palm-lined shores contrast with snow-capped mountains and primeval forests. Favourite hiking destinations are the glacier world of Diablerets, the summit of La Berneuse with its «Le Kuklos» revolving restaurant and the Rochers de Naye with perfect vistas across Lake Geneva. Panorama trains, aerial cableways and cogwheel railways ensure that you can climb in comfort. And you can also probe the subterranean world. The Orbe caves,

with their stalactites and stalagmites, are among the most beautiful in Europe and «white gold» is still won from the salt mines in Bex.

Stepping into the history-steeped towns is to take a journey through time. Noviodunum, Nyon, holds precious remains from Roman times and the castles in Rolles and Morges date from the 13th and 15th centuries. The thermal spas at Yverdon-les-Bains were appreciated by the ancient Romans many centuries ago. About 50 museums take visitors on journeys into past and present, from the Olympic Museum in Lausanne to the Watch & Clock Museum in Vallée de Joux.

In 2007, the lovely, terraced landscape of the Lavaux wine-growing area was added to the prestigious list of Unesco World Heritage sites. The vineyard trail is a journey of discovery through a manmade cultural landscape. Welcoming wine cellars and restaurants extend invitations to taste wines and enjoy local specialties such as Vaud Saucisson sausage, Kohlwurst sausage and cheese dishes. But back to hiking: where to start? The trails of the ViaJacobi, the ViaFrancigena, the Via Alpina, the Alpenpanoramaweg, the Jura-Höhenweg and the Alpenpässe-Weg all pass by here, and so many 'highlight routes' promise exclusive hiking pleasure.

Perhaps you should simply start with the Uferweg, the walk along the shores between Montreux and Vevey in the footsteps of famous guests. Not only Johann Wolfgang von Goethe felt at home on Lake Geneva. Chillon Castle inspired Lord Byron to write his sonnet «The Prisoner of Chillon», and many other prominent persons have strolled along the lakeside promenade, including Ernest Hemingway, Rainer Maria Rilke and Leo Tolstoi, Fjodor Dostojewski, Victor Hugo and Sissi, Empress of Austria. A statue of Charlie Chaplin stands in Vevey, in Montreux a statue of Freddie Mercury, who once sang «This could be heaven». He surely must have meant the Lake Geneva region…

Moors and more …

A restaurant, a few scattered houses – L'Etivaz. But here, almost at the end of the world, you find the modern centre of administration, culture, tourism and sales for L'Etivaz AOC, produced on the surrounding alps in summer. 22 000 cheese wheels are stored here and then sold as far afield as Paris and New York. A multivision show is presented in the show dairy. Several cows who are responsible for this cheese gaze quizzically at the hikers along this moorland area leading to La Lécherette. At the Lécherette Restaurant you share the tables with cyclists and motorcyclists.

Gently undulating alps shape the topography around the Hongrin reservoir. Mont d'Or, Tour d'Aï, Pointe d'Aveneyre and Rochers de Naye, together with the Lac de l'Hongrin form a breathtaking panorama from the Höhenstrasse road. Pigs, goats and cows share common sleeping quarters and provide highly original photographic subjects.

The steep terrain after the Linderrey Pass is difficult to farm, as the remains of an alp hut prove. The metres lost in height are regained on the ever-changing ascent to the remarkable Rochers de Naye.

Alp La Vuichoude d'en Bas

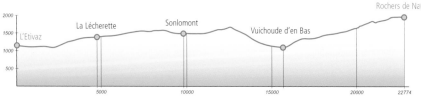

Ascent to Col de
Chaude

Rochers de Naye,
south ridge

The narrow, uphill trail from Col de Chaude on steep grassy slopes and the subsequent ridge at 2000 metres open up views to Lake Geneva and from the Eiger to Mont-blanc. On its south side, the Rochers de Naye is bordered by mighty cliffs but access is well made and easy. Six fully equipped Mongolian yurts at the summit station offer unusual overnight accommodation.

L'Etivaz		0:00	🚌🚐✕🏕🛒	9 h	🕐
La Lécherette	1:45	1:45	🚐✕🏕🛒	22,8 km	↔
Sonlomont	1:35	3:20	✳	1810 m	↗
Vuichoude d'en Bas	2:10	5:30		995 m	↘
Rochers de Naye	3:30	9:00	🚌🚐✕🏕✳	high	🚶
				262 T Rochers de Naye	🗺

Fascinating ridge hike

It's an unbelievably sublime feeling to look back from the spectacular Rochers de Naye to the trail that you've just hiked. Hundreds of rocky peaks and summits soar up on the horizon and Lake Geneva and its chic shores lie peacefully below the morning haze. You can stroke the usually shy marmots in their enclosures. A garden of plants gives an insight into the rich variety of Alpine flora. The fascinating rock restaurant on the north side of the mountain is linked to the summit station via a tunnel. Up here on the terrace, even the less fit can marvel at Montreux and the steep rock faces of the Rochers du Naye. The trail towards the west along the steep south slope and a further ridge is the last

true highlight of the Via Alpina. Then follows a section cut into a sandstone cliff face. It affords dizzyingly deep views but is wide and well secured with a solid wooden balustrade. At Liboson d'en Haut, a marble slab with a panorama etched into it

Rochers de Naye, west ridge

provides information on the Savoyan Alps. In Caux, the striking «castle» of the Swiss Hotel Management School is visible from afar; an eye-catching, art-nouveau building with numerous towers, built in the heyday of

Alp Sautodoz

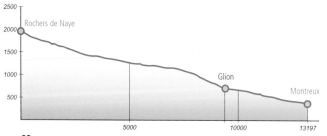

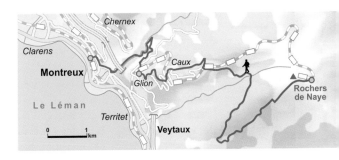

Hotel Management School in Caux

19th century tourism. Montreux is blessed with a Mediterranean climate, much appreciated by its multitude of famous and wealthy guests. The jazz town offers first-class hotels, concert halls, a breath of

B. B. King, Freddie Mercury and Miles Davis, and an endless promenade.

Rochers de Naye		0:00	🚡 219 🚍 ✕ 🏠 ☀	4 h 55 min	🕐
Glion	3:25	3:25	🚡 🚌 ✕ 🏠 🚃 ☀	13,2 km	↔
Montreux	1:30	4:55	🚂 🚍 ⛴ 🚃 ✕ 🏠 🚃	295 m	↗
				1880 m	↘
				medium	🚶
				262 T Rochers de Naye	🏞

BeeTagg list

For an explanation on BeeTaggs see pages 14–15.

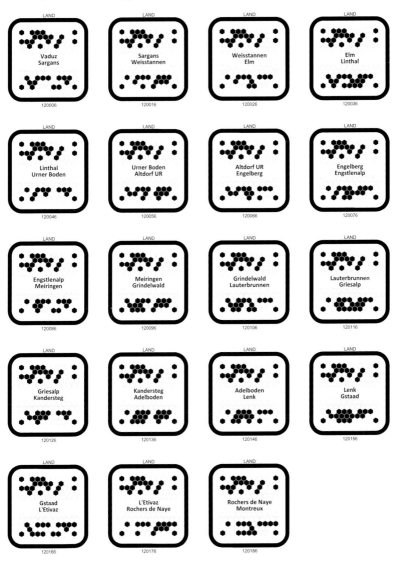

Raus. Aber richtig.

Schweizer Wanderwege
Suisse Rando
Sentieri Svizzeri
Sendas Svizras

Werden Sie Gönnerin / Gönner der Schweizer Wanderwege

Die Schweizer Wanderwege sorgen gemeinsam mit den kantonalen Wanderweg-Fachorganisationen dafür, dass Sie Ih Wanderungen in der Schweiz so richtig geniessen können.

Damit wir als gemeinnützige Organisationen die vielfältigen Aufgaben rund um die Wanderwege und zur Förderung des Wanderns wahrnehmen können, sind wir auf Ihre finanzielle Unterstützung angewiesen.

Wir würden uns sehr freuen, wenn wir Sie zum Kreis unserer Gönnerinnen und Gönner zählen dürften. Jeder finanzielle Beitrag ist herzlich willkommen.

Exklusive Leistungen für Gönnerinnen und Gönner der Schweizer Wanderweg

- Rund 20% Rabatt auf sämtlichen Wanderbüchern und Wanderkarten in unserem Wander-Shop (www.shop.wandern.ch)
- Zustellung des Wandergutscheinheftes «Wandern mit Bonus» im März
- Zustellung eines Wanderführers mit 10 Wandervorschlägen zu einem besonderen Thema im September
- 10% Rabatt auf dem Sortiment (mit wenigen Ausnahmen) des Outdoor-Versandhauses Sirius in Herzogenbuchsee (www.sirius-outdoor.ch)

Anmeldungen an:
Schweizer Wanderwege, Monbijoustrasse 61, 3011 Bern
Tel. 031 370 10 20 / Fax 031 370 10 21
Mail: info@wandern.ch / www.wandern.ch

Für die Natur gerüstet.

40-mal SportXX in der Schweiz.

SPORTXX

MIGROS